First published 1997 by University of Queensland Press
Reprinted 2004, 2005, 2007, 2010
This edition first published 2020 by SILKIM BOOKS
PO Box 693, Ballina, New South Wales 2478 Australia

Designed by Kim Michelle Toft
Graphic design and layout by Peter Evans
Printed by Everbest Printing Co. Ltd. China

A catalogue record for this
work is available from the
NATIONAL LIBRARY OF AUSTRALIA    National Library of Australia

ISBN 978 0 9942388 5 6 (pbk)

*This book is dedicated to Casey Elle
and her children and their children & their children...
Special thanks to our Mums, Beryl and Gloria and our friend Lesley Henry.*

**Kim Michelle Toft** is a full-time silk artist. One Less Fish, her first book, is a reflection of her love for the tropical paradise of Far North Queensland and her desire to help the next generation understand the importance of its preservation.
**Allan Sheather** was born in Mullumbimby and grew up surfing the beaches of Byron Bay. He is a popular local character who still plays footy with his local club.

# One less fish

Kim Michelle Toft and Allan Sheather
Illustrations by Kim Michelle Toft

**silkim**
BOOKS

12     twelve

Twelve gracious angelfish
thinking they're in heaven.
Along came the divers
now there are ...

# 11

eleven.

Spear fishing and scuba diving are popular sports, although today many divers only look at or photograph fish and do not kill them.

Eleven cheeky snapper
racing round the bend.
One took a hook
now there's only ...

# 10 ten.

 Recreational fishing, or fishing for fun, has always been a popular pastime. People who fish must be careful not to catch too many, and if they catch undersized fish they should put them back into the ocean.

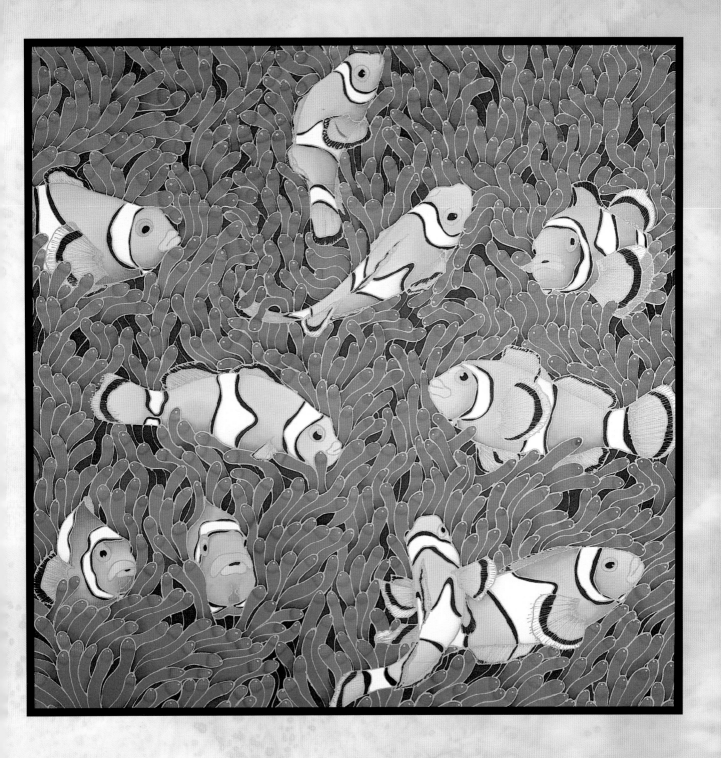

Ten dainty clownfish
wondering where to dine.
People started drilling
now there's only ...

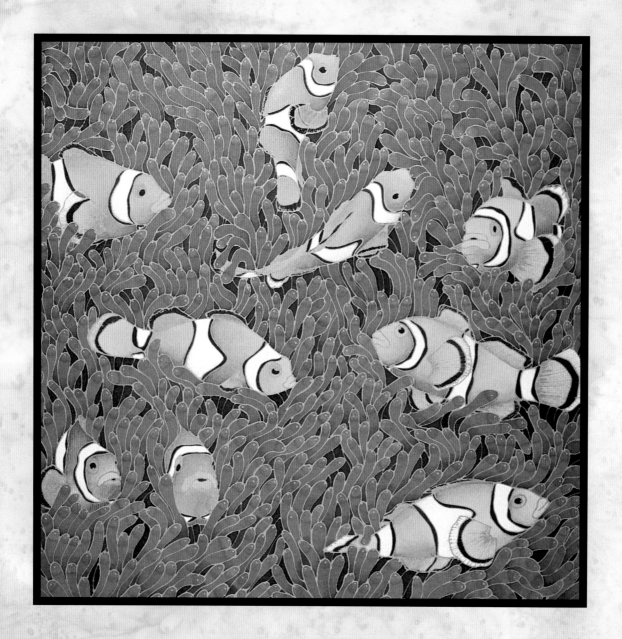

9

nine.

Drilling for oil takes place on, or close to some reefs throughout the world; fortunately not on the Great Barrier Reef. Oil leaks can occur, damaging reef **ecosystems**. Many reefs around the world are mined for building materials and reefs cannot **regenerate**.

Nine tiny triggerfish
wonderfully ornate.
Didn't see the plastic bag
now there's only …

8

eight.

Each day large amounts of rubbish are tipped into the ocean. Some modern materials do not **disintegrate**. Turtles and whales sometimes think plastic bags are jellyfish and swallow them. Fish, birds, turtles and seals are often caught in plastic material and choke to death.

Eight weary wrasse
fed by naughty Kevin.
Shouldn't feed the fish
now there's only …

# 7     seven.

Feeding fish different and unusual food can be dangerous. It upsets their diet and may even poison them.

Seven pretty parrotfish
performing silly tricks.
One ignored a fish net
now there's only ...

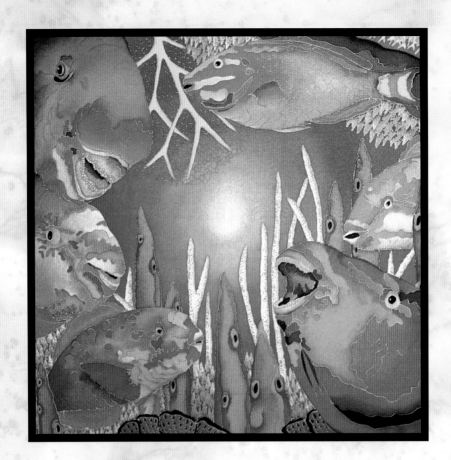

# 6

six.

Over-fishing can mean that not enough fish are left to breed in proper numbers. Some fish caught in commercial fishing nets are not even wanted by the fisherman.

Six striking tuskfish
glad to be alive.
Pesticides have killed one
now there's only ...

5 five.

**Pesticides** spread on the land can seep into rivers and the sea. They do not break down in the water and can build up in the **food chain**, poisoning sea creatures.

Five moorish idols
longing to explore.
The water's getting muddy
now there's only …

# 4

four.

Coral needs light to be able to grow. If a lot of **silt** runs off into the ocean around the reef it makes the water muddy stopping the light reaching the coral. This is often caused by clearing large areas of vegetation along the coastline.

Four coral cod
behind a coral tree.
A tanker had an oil spill
now there's only …

# 3

## three.

Damaged ships can leak oil into the sea. Birds, fish and other sea life, including plants and coral, can be smothered by the oil and die.

Three fairy basslets
swimming into view.
Crashing anchors break their home
now there's only ...

2     two.

Boats anchoring in the wrong areas of the reef can cause damage by dragging their anchors and breaking off large chunks of coral.

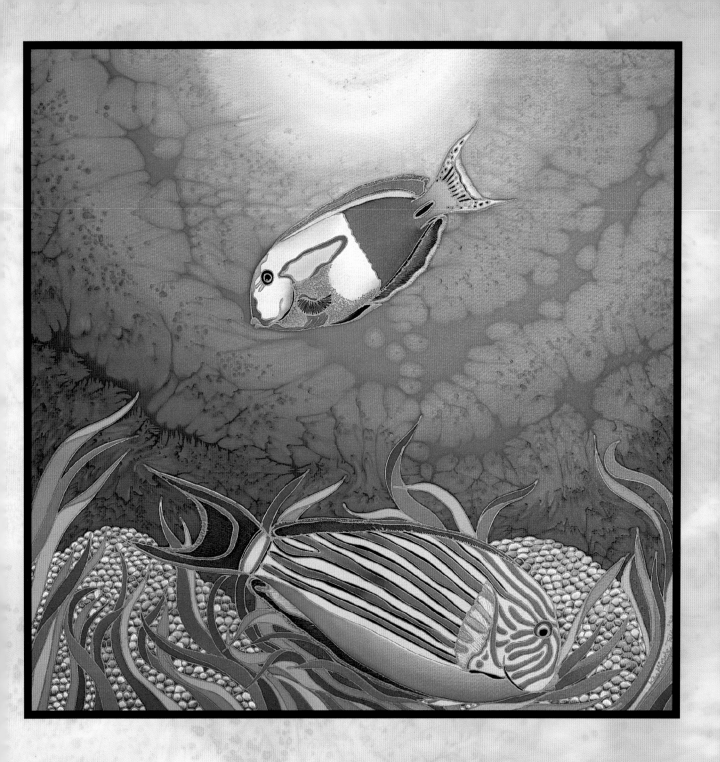

Two hungry surgeonfish
not having any fun.
Little left to eat
now there's only ...

# 1

## one.

If the reef **ecosystem** is destroyed there will be nothing left for sea creatures to live on.

One lonely lionfish
left to be the hero.
No fish left to save
now there is ...

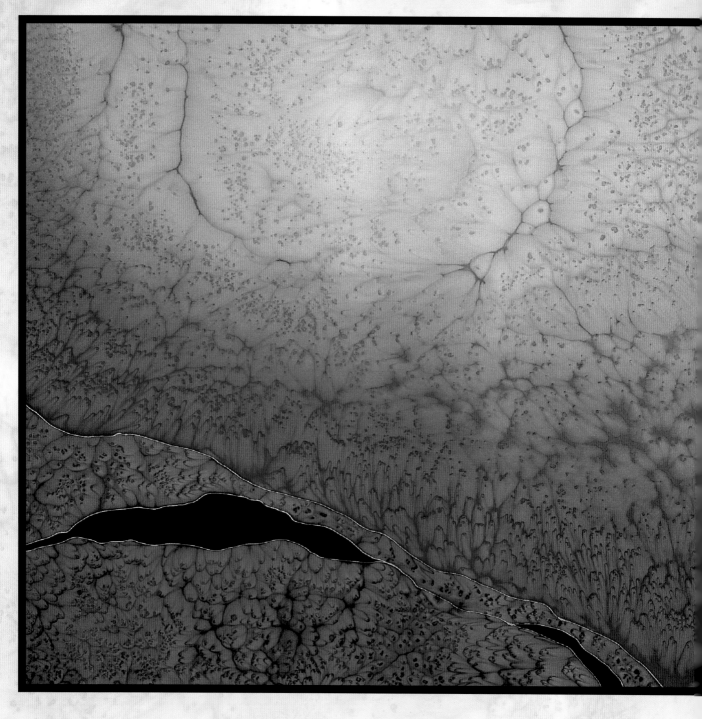

0   zero.

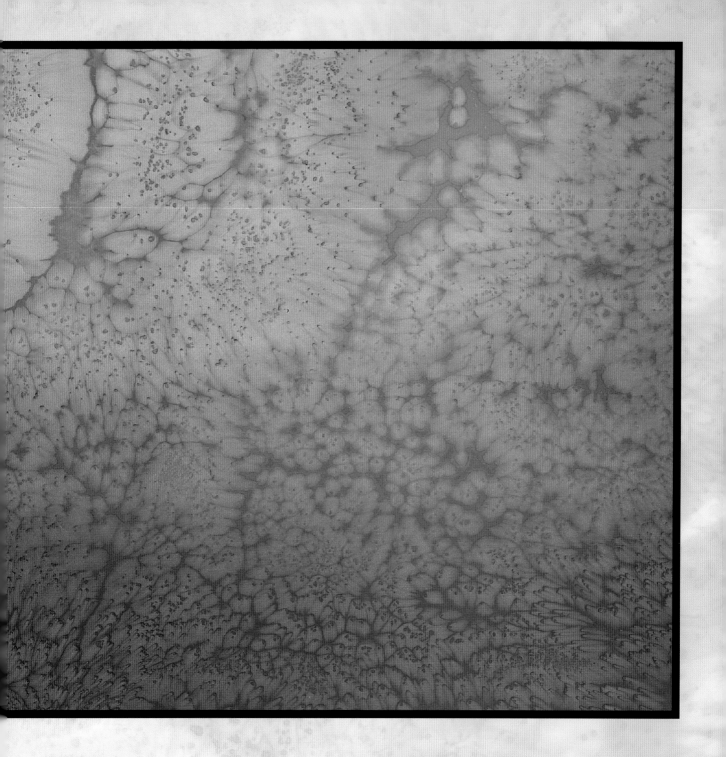

Without constant care we will lose some
of the world's most beautiful natural resources.
Remember: fish that die one by one
may soon become none by none.